MW01002577

NATIONAL TRUST

Book of
Puddings

NATIONAL TRUST

Book of
Puddings

Regula Ysewijn

National Trust

First published in the United Kingdom in 2019 by
National Trust Books
43 Great Ormond Street
London
WC1N 3HZ

An imprint of Pavilion Books Group Ltd

Volume © National Trust Books, 2019
Text © Regula Ysewijn, 2019
Illustrations by Louise Morgan

The moral rights of the author have been asserted. All rights reserved.
No part of this publication may be reproduced, stored in a retrieval
system, or transmitted in any form or by any means electronic,
mechanical, photocopying, recording or otherwise, without the prior
written permission of the copyright owner.

ISBN: 9781911358589

A CIP catalogue record for this book is available from the British
Library.

10 9 8 7 6 5 4

Reproduction by Rival Colour Ltd, UK
Printed and bound by Toppan Leefung Printing Ltd, China

This book can be ordered direct from the publisher at the website:
www.pavilionbooks.com, or try your local bookshop. Also available at
National Trust shops or www.nationaltrustbooks.co.uk

Contents

Introduction

When the National Trust asked me to write this book, I was delighted. As an Anglophile I've done extensive research into British food culture and history for the past 15 years and the iconic puddings in particular intrigued me to say the least. I dived into my centuries-old cookery books in search of what really constitutes a pudding. I savoured the forgotten flavour combinations, the creative use of spices, the harmony and the blurred line between sweet and savoury that defines the heritage of pudding.

When I put the word out that I wanted to hear about everyone's favourites, pudding aficionados from all over the country and beyond contacted me about their much-loved desserts, often the ones they ate in school many years ago, or the ones their parents and grandparents used to serve. These 50 cockle-warming recipes were partly chosen by the many people who sent me their suggestions or pleas to search for a recipe long-lost but very much treasured in their memories.

Pudding is deeply rooted in the British psyche; it is part of what it means to be British and it has been that way for centuries. When the pudding cloth was invented in the fifteenth century – meaning that puddings no longer needed to be boiled in animal innards – there was scope for many new pudding recipes. By the seventeenth century a French visitor, François Maximilien Misson, noted the delights of pudding in his travel diary: 'Blessed be he that invented pudding, for it is a manna that hits the palates of all sorts of people; a manna better than that of the wilderness, because the people are never weary of it. Ah, what an excellent thing is an English pudding!'

Roast beef accompanied by plum pudding became the national dish, and during the Napoleonic wars it was served as a statement of loyalty to the crown. At this time English and French cuisine could not be more different. French food culture was defined by intricate dishes while British food was straightforward, with an emphasis on products with the best provenance. In one satirical illustration of that time, entitled 'The Plumb-pudding in danger', British Prime Minister William Pitt and Napoleon are greedily carving up a steaming pudding representing the globe with fork and sabre – Napoleon eagerly cutting off Europe, his eyes firmly on the prize.

In Victorian times a plum pudding became the icon of togetherness and family. It featured on the first printed Christmas cards, lovingly placed in the middle of a festive table. It was puddings for all in the nineteenth century. Plum duff and meat puddings ruled in the streets while impressive jellies and blancmanges entertained the elite. Techniques evolved in cooking as well as in the manufacturing of elaborate pudding moulds.

The Empire Marketing Board was founded in 1926 to promote Empire produce and trade, and in the winter of that year they distributed a recipe for 'Empire Pudding'. The leaflet showed a powerful illustration of Lady Britannia holding a flaming plum pudding topped with a Union Jack. It read 'Buy Empire Goods – Ask – Is it British?'.

You could show your patriotism with your pudding-making. Two world wars and years of rationing made it near-impossible to make the usual puddings at all. After the Second World War, traditional British puddings were replaced by French gateaux and other more dainty looking alternatives on the restaurant menus. Pudding became something you had at home or at school but not in a restaurant. The 1990s brought change, and with chefs like Gary Rhodes and Jamie Oliver, proper British puddings were something to be proud of again; more and more restaurants and gastropubs put pudding back on the menu. Today I can't imagine a day of walking in the British countryside without a warming sticky toffee apple pudding to restore my strength in a village pub. A British meal without a proper pudding is only half a meal in my book.

About the recipes

• All spoon measurements are level, unless specified otherwise.

1 teaspoon = 5ml

1 tablespoon = 15ml

• Eggs are medium, free range, organic if possible.

• Milk is full fat (whole).

• Butter is always unsalted unless specified otherwise.

• Citrus fruit zest is always from unwaxed fruit, organic if possible.

• Spices: please don't use that forgotten jar of cinnamon you found in the back of your cupboard; the flavour will disappoint you as the aroma of spices fades when they are old.

• Oven temperatures are for conventional ovens. If you use a fan oven you may need to reduce the temperature by 10°C.

• Bake on the middle shelf of the oven unless specified otherwise.

• It is not always safe to eat uncooked eggs; this applies to the very young, the elderly, pregnant women, and anyone who is ill or has a weak immune system. When a meringue is not baked in the oven the recipe calls for pasteurised egg whites, which you can buy in some supermarkets and health food shops. Alternatively you'll need to make an Italian meringue, using a sugar syrup to cook the egg whites. To make a sugar syrup for a meringue with 5 egg whites, combine 300g of caster sugar and 80g of water in a saucepan; put a sugar thermometer in the pan and heat to 110°C then reduce the heat and let it bubble gently until the temperature goes up to 120°C. Meanwhile, whisk your egg whites to stiff peaks in a stand mixer. Start adding the syrup to the egg whites while continuously whisking on a low speed. When all the syrup is in, leave the mixer beating at a low speed for a further 5 minutes until thick and glossy.

How to cook a pudding

———o———————————o———

The earliest puddings were made in bag-like animal stomachs or intestines, just as haggis and some sausages are today. From stomach to the stuffed uterus popular in Roman cooking, if you could stuff it, it was stuffed with meat or offal, grains and dried fruits. 'Sweet herbs' were used as flavouring; I am sure that to our medieval ancestors a pudding was so special because it had sweet notes during a time when sugar was almost unobtainable.

The pudding cloth first appeared in the fifteenth century; as a result pudding-making became possible outside slaughter time, and puddings became more popular. An array of meatless puddings was born. By the eighteenth century, pudding chapters in books were extensive, with recipes both sweet and savoury. Some form of pudding was eaten with every course of the meal.

Fancy copper or ceramic moulds for jellies and steamed puddings in the shape of fish, swans, fruit or ornate buildings became fashionable from the mid-eighteenth century and into the nineteenth. To impress your guests with all sorts of pudding was to be the perfect host. In the twentieth century pudding became synonymous with dessert, the last course of a meal. Yet you can still have pudding in each course: a batter pudding for the first course, a steak and kidney pudding for your main, and a sticky toffee pudding for dessert. And what about a spinach pudding as a side dish?

If you like, you can boil a pudding in a cloth, but do soak your cloth or tea towel in boiling water before use. I find it more practical to use a plain pudding basin. I prefer to steam a pudding in a pan in the oven rather than on the hob. It is much safer than leaving a gigantic pot of simmering water on the stove for hours on end, but remember to check from time to time whether you need to top up the pan with hot water.

To prepare your pudding for steaming

Preheat the oven to 160°C.

Cut a circle of baking paper to fit the bottom of the pudding basin and two larger circles with a diameter about 10cm larger than the top of the basin. Bring a kettle of water to the boil.

Generously grease the pudding basin and place the small circle of baking paper in the bottom, then spoon in the mixture. Placing the two larger circles of baking paper together, make a narrow fold across the middle to allow the paper cover to expand slightly as the pudding does. Tie securely around the top of the basin with kitchen string and tie the string to create a handle so it will be easier to lift the pudding out when it is ready. Place a trivet or an inverted saucer on the bottom of a large deep pan and place the pudding basin on top so the steam can circulate. Pour in boiling water to come halfway up the side of the basin. Cover the pan, either with its own lid or with foil, in order to trap the steam. Place in the oven and leave for as long as your recipe states.

When your pudding is done, be careful while removing it from the pan of hot water and when removing the wrapping. To unmould, place a plate on top of the basin, wrap in a tea towel and invert to turn the pudding out on to the plate.

Steamed Puddings

Sticky Date and Butterscotch Puddings

A comforting pudding from Berrington Hall in Herefordshire.

140g stoned dates, chopped
150ml boiling water
½ teaspoon bicarbonate of soda
55g butter
55g soft dark brown sugar
1 egg

85g self-raising flour
FOR THE BUTTERSCOTCH SAUCE
85g light brown sugar
25g salted butter
150ml single cream

Lightly butter four 200ml pudding moulds and line the bottoms with a circle of baking paper.

Put the dates in a saucepan with the water and bicarbonate of soda and stir until the soda is dissolved. Add the butter and sugar and cook for a few minutes until the dates are soft enough to beat to a purée.

Remove the pan from the heat and quickly beat in the egg and flour until well mixed.

Divide the mixture evenly between the prepared pudding moulds. Cover with buttered foil and steam for about 1 hour or until well risen and a skewer comes out cleanly when inserted into the centre of one of the puddings.

While the puddings cook, make the sauce. Add the sugar and 2 tablespoons of water to a small saucepan, heat gently without stirring until the sugar has dissolved then boil for a few minutes until it begins to smell of toffee. Take off the heat and carefully stir in the butter then the cream until smooth.

Using the tip of a knife or spatula, loosen the edges of the puddings then turn out on to plates. Spoon over the sauce and serve with vanilla ice cream or custard.

Dolbury Pudding

This recipe is from Killerton, an eighteenth-century family house in the east Devon countryside. This steamed pudding appears in *Classic British Cooking*, where Sarah Edington explains that the pudding was named after the rounded shape of Dolbury Hill, which can be seen behind the house. All puddings steamed in traditional pudding basins look like hills but it's a great idea to actually name one after a hill.

110g butter
25g lard
150g soft brown sugar
3 eggs, beaten
200g apples, weighed when peeled
   and chopped

200g mincemeat
225g self-raising flour, sifted
A little milk if required

Grease a 1.2–1.5 litre pudding basin or 6 individual pudding basins. Put a round of greased greaseproof paper in the bottom of each.

Cream together the butter, lard and sugar until pale and fluffy. Add the beaten eggs, a little at a time, beating well after each addition. Stir in the apples and mincemeat. Gently fold in the flour. If necessary add a little milk to the mixture to give a soft dropping consistency.

Spoon the mixture into the basins, filling each by two-thirds. Cover the basins loosely with a double layer of greaseproof paper or a piece of foil and secure with string. Steam for 2 hours. For the individual pudding basins follow the cooking instructions for the Steamed Lemon Sponge Puddings on page 24.

Turn out on to a plate and serve with custard or cream.

Cabinet Pudding

This pudding is also sometimes called diplomat pudding or
Newcastle pudding. Leftover cake – and biscuits, if you like – is
layered with glacé cherries and steeped in an egg custard mixture
before steaming. The joys of using up stale cake in a household
where the last bit of cake is always left in the tin! I bag the stale
cake and put it in the freezer until I have enough to make a
pudding. The outside of the pudding is traditionally decorated
with candied orange, cherries or angelica, and you can do this by
sticking the fruit to the buttered mould before filling.

200g stale sponge cake
10–15 amaretti biscuits (optional)
Brandy or dark rum, to taste
15 glacé cherries

FOR THE CUSTARD
5 egg yolks
250ml milk
250ml double cream
25g caster sugar
1 vanilla pod, split
1 tablespoon cornflour

Preheat the oven to 180°C.

Slice the sponge cake into 1cm thick pieces and arrange in a deep
plate, with the biscuits if using. Drizzle with a generous amount of
brandy or rum and leave to soak.

To make the custard, whisk the egg yolks in a large bowl. In a
saucepan, bring the milk, cream, sugar and vanilla pod to a simmer.
Remove the vanilla pod and pour a little of the hot cream mixture
into the egg yolks while whisking vigorously, then add the cornflour
and whisk until completely dissolved. Continue to add the cream
mixture bit by bit, whisking until smooth. Pour the mixture back into
the saucepan and cook over a low heat until the custard thickens. Let
it cool slightly while you fill the mould.

Lightly butter a 1.2-litre mould. Place a few cherries in the base of the mould, then add a layer of sponge cake and one of biscuits, then add a few more cherries and another layer of sponge and biscuits. Repeat until the mould is three-quarters full.

Pour in the lukewarm custard then place the mould on a trivet or an inverted saucer in a large, deep pan. Cover the mould with foil, then pour in boiling water to come halfway up the side of the mould. Put the lid on the pan and carefully put the pan in the oven. Steam for 1 hour.

Allow the pudding to cool in the mould for 5 minutes before turning out on to a plate. Serve immediately.

Prince Albert Pudding

This pudding was designed by Charles Elmé Francatelli who was, for a very short period, Queen Victoria and Prince Albert's head chef. This recipe appears in his 1846 book, *The Modern Chef*. It is a relatively plain recipe for a royal menu, which suggests it was intended for the Prince who, according to historian Annie Gray, preferred food that was not highly flavoured and easy to digest.

170g leftover pound cake or Madeira
    cake, crumbled
120ml single cream
2 egg yolks
1 egg white, whisked to soft peaks
Grated zest of ½ lemon
110g caster sugar

Preheat the oven to 160°C.

Prepare a 1-litre cake tin for steaming (page 11).

Put the cake crumbs in a large bowl, add the cream and leave to soak for about 15 minutes. Add the eggs, lemon zest and sugar and combine well.

Pour the mixture into the pudding basin, cover with baking paper or foil and secure with string. Steam in the oven for 50 minutes.

Turn out on to a plate and serve with custard.

Spotted Dick

Spotted dick was a popular street food with the working-class people of Victorian London. It was cooked in big steaming kettles and children knew exactly which vendor sold the spotted dick that had the most currants in it. The pudding is also knows as spotted dog or Alma pudding.

150g currants
4 tablespoons (approx.) water, brandy
   or rum (optional)
300g plain flour
130g shredded suet

100g demerara sugar
1 teaspoon ground cinnamon
1 teaspoon baking powder
1 egg
200ml milk

Preheat the oven to 160°C.

Prepare a 2-litre pudding basin for steaming (page 11). Put the currants in a bowl and cover with a little water, brandy or rum.

Combine the flour, suet, sugar, cinnamon and baking powder together in a large bowl and mix well. Add the egg and the milk in batches until you can bring the mixture together to form a stiff dough, using your hands or a wooden spoon. If it is too dry, you might need another splash of milk, although the dough should not be too wet or sticky.

Drain the currants and pat them dry with kitchen towel. Add the currants to the dough.

Roll the dough into a ball and press into the prepared pudding basin. Cover the pudding and steam in the oven for 4 hours.

Turn out and serve with ladlefuls of custard.

Sussex Pond Pudding

The modern version of this pudding is made with a lemon in
the centre but it was originally made by stuffing the dough with
apples or gooseberries. The oldest recipe for a Sussex pudding
dates from 1672 and was published in *The Queen-like Closet* by
Hannah Wolley.

FOR THE SUET CRUST
300g self-raising flour
130g shredded suet
½ teaspoon ground cinnamon
Pinch of salt
2 teaspoons lemon juice
Grated zest of ½ lemon
70ml single cream, chilled

FOR THE FILLING
440g dessert apple, peeled and cubed
140g light brown sugar
½ teaspoon ground cinnamon
150g butter, cubed, chilled

Preheat the oven to 160°C.

Prepare two 1.2-litre pudding basins for steaming (page 11).

In a large bowl, mix the flour with the suet, cinnamon and salt. Then
add the lemon juice, zest, cream and 120ml of cold water to bring the
mixture together to form a stiff dough.

Roll out the dough on a lightly floured surface and keep one-quarter
of the dough aside for the lids. Line the pudding basins with the
dough, gently pressing it down and moulding it so it is roughly the
same thickness all over.

To make the filling, mix the apple with the sugar and cinnamon
until all the apple is well coated, then add the cubes of butter and
mix evenly.

Divide the apple mixture between the pudding basins. Fit a lid of dough to each pudding and crimp the edges well to seal the puddings. Cover the puddings and steam in the oven for 3 hours.

Turn out on to deep plates to catch the buttery juices.

VARIATION Add blackberries to the apples for a different flavour and added colour.

Autumn Hedgerow Pudding

A perfect way to use blackberries and elderberries. Using frozen blackberries is fine; freeze when you have plenty, or buy frozen. The recipe for elderberry jam makes much more than you need; this tart jam goes well with cheese and can also be used in the Manchester Tart (page 56) and the Cornflake Tart (page 50).

130g butter
120g demerara sugar
1 teaspoon mixed spice
3 eggs
Grated zest and juice of ½ lemon
25g ground almonds
155g plain flour
½ teaspoon baking powder
125g blackberries

FOR THE ELDERBERRY JAM
500g elderberries
500g jam sugar
Juice of ½ lemon

First, make the jam; put a saucer in the freezer to test the jam set. Remove the elderberries from the stems and put the berries into a deep saucepan. Add a splash of water and cook the fruit until it is soft, then strain to remove the little pips. Add the sugar to the strained juice and bring to the boil for 5 minutes. Test if the jam is set by putting a small blob of jam on the saucer you put in the freezer: push it with your finger and it should form a wrinkled skin. If not, keep boiling and repeat the process every few minutes until the jam is set.

Preheat the oven to 180°C.

Prepare a 1-litre pudding basin for steaming (page 11).

Beat the butter, sugar and spice together until light and creamy.
Add the eggs, one at a time, with the lemon juice and zest, beating
thoroughly. Fold in the almonds, sift in the flour and baking powder,
then add two-thirds of the blackberries.

Spoon 2 tablespoons of elderberry jam into the pudding basin then
drop in the last of the blackberries. Dollop half the pudding mixture
on top. Make a little well in the middle and add 1 teaspoon of the jam,
spreading it out but staying away from the edges. Now add the rest of
the mixture and cover the basin.

Steam in the oven for 1½ hours, then check by inserting a toothpick
to see if it comes out clean; if not, continue steaming until the pudding
is done.

Turn out and serve with custard, clotted cream or vanilla ice cream.

VARIATION Add 50g of chopped cooking apple or some more berries
to the batter; the cooking time will need to be increased if you add
more fruit.

Steamed Lemon Sponge Puddings

When it comes to a steamed lemon sponge, I prefer to have my own small individual pudding. You can freeze them in the basins then defrost and reheat in the microwave to be eaten later.

200g butter, softened, plus extra for
    greasing
200g demerera sugar
Grated zest of 1 small lemon

50g candied lemon or citron peel,
    finely chopped
4 eggs
200g self-raising flour
3–4 tablespoons lemon curd

Preheat the oven to 180°C.

Generously butter eight 150ml pudding basins, then cut a disc of baking paper to line the base of each basin.

Beat the butter with the sugar until pale and creamy. Add the grated lemon zest and the candied peel. Add the eggs one at a time, whisking until each egg is fully incorporated. Finally, fold in the flour and combine well.

Dollop 1 teaspoon of lemon curd into each basin. Divide the pudding mixture between the basins until they are about two-thirds full.

Place all the puddings in a deep baking tray and add boiling water to come halfway up the sides of the basins. Cover each basin and the baking tray with foil and steam in the oven for 50 minutes, checking after 40 minutes by inserting a toothpick into a pudding; if it comes out clean the pudding is done.

Using the tip of a knife, loosen the puddings from the basins and turn out on to serving plates. Serve with custard or clotted cream.

Serves 8-10

Ginger Syrup Pudding

A ginger syrup pudding has to have suet in it, although it's just as easily made with just self-raising flour, I want this pudding to have the substance only the suet can provide. It's not a pudding to have every day; it demands a special occasion. Plan ahead and prepare the pudding a day in advance; steam it while you are eating dinner and then all you need to do after dinner is to make a proper custard.

150g plain flour
1 teaspoon baking powder
100g shredded suet
100g fresh white breadcrumbs
155g demerara sugar
1 teaspoon ground cinnamon
½ teaspoon ground nutmeg

Pinch of salt
Pinch of freshly ground black pepper
3 teaspoons grated fresh ginger
3 eggs, beaten
125g golden syrup
3 tablespoons thin-cut marmalade
3 tablespoons ginger preserve

It is best to make the batter a day or a few hours in advance. Place all the dry ingredients in a large bowl and mix well. Add the fresh ginger, then the eggs, one by one, followed by the golden syrup and marmalade. Combine the mixture well.

Prepare a 2-litre pudding basin for steaming (page 11) and preheat the oven to 160°C.

Spoon the ginger preserve into the base of the basin then add the pudding mixture. Cover and steam in the oven for 3 hours.

Turn out and serve with custard or clotted cream.

Figgy Pudding

A figgy pudding is just another name for a plum pudding – and both of them generally refer to puddings made with raisins or currants. This is a dark and luxurious winter pudding. Why not have this as your dessert on Christmas day for a change?

400g dried figs	120g brown sugar
3 tablespoons golden syrup	60g fresh breadcrumbs
120ml red wine	1 teaspoon baking powder
20ml Cointreau	½ teaspoon ground nutmeg
60g currants	1 teaspoon mixed spice
FOR THE PUDDING	Pinch of salt
110g plain flour	2 eggs
60g shredded suet	75ml stout or porter beer

Start the day before you want to make the pudding. Put the figs and golden syrup into a saucepan with the red wine and Cointreau and bring to a simmer for about 5 minutes, stirring to immerse the figs in the liquid. When the figs have softened, remove them and set aside while simmering the liquid until it becomes syrupy. Cut any tough stems off the figs, then halve the figs and put them in the syrup to soak overnight. Soak the currants separately in a little water.

It is also best to mix the pudding a day or a few hours in advance. Mix together all the dry ingredients in a large bowl, then add the eggs, currants and stout and mix well by gently stirring with a wooden spoon.

Prepare a 1.1-litre pudding basin for steaming (page 11) and preheat the oven to 160°C.

Arrange the halved figs all around the basin. Chop any leftover figs and fold them into the pudding mixture then spoon the mixture into the basin, cover and steam in the oven for 3 hours.

When done, turn the pudding out on to a plate. Warm any leftover syrup and drizzle over the pudding. Slice and serve with custard or clotted cream.

St George's Pudding

This recipe was suggested to me by food historian Annie Gray, who is currently researching the life of Georgina Landemare, Churchill's cook at his Kentish home, Chartwell, which is now owned by the National Trust. It's served with a sack sauce – sack being an old word for a fortified wine like a sweetish sherry. The recipe calls for chopped preserved fruit, meaning soft candied fruit in syrup, much like Greek spoon fruits. If you can't get your hands on those, glacé cherries work well too.

1 Savoy cake (page 66), baked in a
    cake tin
170g butter
80g demerara sugar
Grated zest of 1 lemon
60g shredded suet
30g cornflour
4 eggs, separated
150g preserved fruit in syrup or glacé
    cherries

FOR THE SACK SAUCE
100g butter
100g light brown sugar
100ml medium sherry

Two days in advance, make the Savoy cake.

To cook the pudding, butter a large cake tin, ideally a ring mould such as a savarin mould or bundt pan, and preheat the oven to 160°C. Cut a piece of Savoy cake weighing 170g and crush it.

Beat the butter and sugar together until creamy then add the lemon zest, suet and cornflour. Beat in the four egg yolks and mix well. Now add the crushed Savoy cake, beating until combined. Whisk your egg whites to stiff peaks and fold into the batter in batches – before adding the last batch, tip in the fruit and then add the last of the egg white, making sure the batter is combined well but taking care not to lose too much air.

If using a ring mould you can place it directly on the bottom of the deep pan as the steam will flow through underneath the mould. If using a cake tin, place on an inverted plate. Cover with foil or baking paper and steam in the oven for 2½ hours. If using a regular cake tin rather than a ring mould your pudding might benefit from 30 minutes more in the oven; test by inserting a toothpick; if it comes out clean your pudding is done.

While the pudding is cooking, make the sack sauce. In a small saucepan, melt the butter until it starts to brown, then add the sugar and sherry and stir until the sugar has dissolved and the sauce is creamy.

Turn out the pudding and serve with the sauce.

Sticky Toffee Apple Puddings

The National Trust's St Michael's Mount in Cornwall once served a sticky toffee apple pudding as part of their Christmas celebrations – seeing this inspired me to create these little puddings. They are light as clouds, but the toffee sauce is deliciously rich.

125g pitted prunes

220g eating apples, peeled, cored and cubed in 1cm pieces

100g soft butter

130g demerara sugar

3 eggs

Pinch of salt

150g plain flour

1 teaspoon baking powder

1 teaspoon mixed spice

Chopped roasted pecans, pistachios and/or hazelnuts, to serve (optional)

FOR THE TOFFEE SAUCE

50g butter

75g brown sugar

75ml double cream

Pinch of sea salt flakes

Soak the prunes in freshly boiled water for 10 minutes, then drain them for at least 5 minutes.

Preheat the oven to 180°C.

Butter six small pudding basins and place a disc of baking paper in the base of each.

In a food processor blitz the soaked prunes to a rough purée.

Beat the butter and sugar together until creamy then add the eggs one at a time, whisking until well combined. Add the prune purée and the salt then fold in the flour, baking powder and spice. Add the apple pieces and stir well.

Spoon the mixture into the pudding basins, filling them three-quarters full. Cover the basins with foil or baking paper, secure with kitchen string and place in a deep baking tray. Pour in boiling water to come roughly halfway up the basins then cover the tray with foil. Steam in the oven for 40–50 minutes, checking after 30 minutes by inserting a toothpick into a pudding; if it comes out clean the puddings are done.

While the puddings steam, make the toffee sauce: melt the butter in a saucepan, add the sugar and cream, bring to the boil and simmer until the sugar has dissolved and the sauce thickens. Add the salt.

When the puddings are done, take them out of their moulds one by one, and dip them carefully in the toffee sauce. Serve with more of the toffee sauce and some chopped roasted nuts if you like.

Syrup Sponge, or Treacle Pudding

Treacle, or molasses, is a by-product of sugar refining and has been used in British cakes for centuries. In the early 1880s the British manufacturer Lyle's began to produce another treacle – golden syrup – and this was used to make syrup sponge and treacle tart.

150g plain flour
1 teaspoon baking powder
60g shredded suet
50g dark brown sugar
40g golden syrup, plus 3 tablespoons for the basin

Pinch of salt
¼ teaspoon ground allspice
1 egg
100ml buttermilk
2 handfuls of pecans

Preheat the oven to 180°C.

Prepare a 1.1-litre pudding basin for steaming (page 11).

Combine the flour, baking powder, suet and sugar together in a large bowl, then add the golden syrup, salt and allspice followed by the egg and the buttermilk. Mix well to combine, then fold through the pecans, keeping back five to line the mould.

Pour the extra 3 tablespoons of golden syrup into the prepared basin then place the five pecans in a star shape in the bottom of the basin. Pour the mixture into the basin, cover and steam in the oven for 1½ hours, checking after 1¼ hours by inserting a toothpick into the pudding; if it comes out clean the pudding is done.

Using the tip of a knife, loosen around the side of the pudding, then turn out the pudding on to a plate. Serve with custard.

Waddesdon Manor Christmas Pudding

This Christmas pudding was served at Waddesdon Manor in Buckinghamshire to James Armand de Rothschild and his wife, Dorothy, in 1939. Although this was a time of wartime shortages they still seemed to have had a good supply of sugar, spices, alcohol and eggs.

225g suet
115g plain flour
225g white breadcrumbs, toasted
450g raisins
115g sultanas
115g currants
225g apple, grated
225g dark brown sugar
85g thick-cut marmalade
5 eggs
2 tablespoons milk
55g almonds, chopped
½ teaspoon salt

1 teaspoon ground cinnamon
1 teaspoon grated nutmeg
1 teaspoon powdered cloves
½ teaspoon baking powder
Grated zest and juice of ½ lemon
4 tablespoons rum
4 tablespoons barley wine or
    strong ale
FOR THE BRANDY BUTTER
175g soft butter
5 tablespoons icing sugar
4 tablespoons brandy

Generously butter two 1.2-litre pudding basins.

Mix all the ingredients together and fill the pudding basins with the mixture. Top with a buttered disc of greaseproof paper and wrap the basins in a double layer of foil to make them watertight.

Steam or boil for 6 hours, topping up with boiling water when necessary.

To make the brandy butter, cream the butter with the sugar and gradually beat in the brandy. Spoon into a small bowl and refrigerate until set.

Turn out the pudding and serve with brandy butter.

Baked Puddings

Apple Dappy

An apple dappy is made like a roly-poly filled with chopped apple and sugar, cut into rounds then laid flat with the swirl upwards. It is a pudding from the West Country.

500g plain white flour

70g demerara sugar

5g salt

225ml milk

15g dried yeast

60g soft butter

1 egg, beaten

1 egg, beaten, for brushing

FOR THE SPREAD

45g brown sugar

70g butter

2 teaspoons ground cinnamon

FOR THE FILLING

500g eating apples, peeled and cored

30g brown sugar

30g butter

Chop the apple into ½–1cm pieces. Stew the apples with the butter and sugar for about 5–8 minutes on a low heat until the fruit is soft but not reduced to a mush. Leave to cool.

Preheat the oven to 200°C.

Line a 24–26cm round baking tin with baking paper.

Place the flour, sugar and salt in the bowl of a mixer. Heat the milk until it is lukewarm and add the yeast; stir to dissolve. Add the butter and half the milk to the dry ingredients and beat with the dough hook. Add the egg and then gradually add the rest of the milk. Knead on medium speed for 5 minutes; the dough will appear quite wet but don't add flour, it will sort itself out while rising. Cover the bowl with clingfilm or a tea towel and leave to rest until doubled in size, usually about an hour.

Meanwhile make the spread that will keep the filling in place. Whisk the butter, sugar and cinnamon together until creamy and set aside at room temperature until you're ready to assemble the rolls.

Turn out your dough on to a lightly floured sheet of baking paper, press into a rectangle and then roll out to 1cm thickness.

Using a spatula, spread the soft cinnamon spread over the dough in a thin layer. Arrange the apple mixture over the spread and roll up, using the baking paper to help you. Slice the roll into six or seven slices and place in the lined baking tin.

Brush with beaten egg and bake for 40-45 minutes or until it is golden brown.

Tear off the pieces and serve with clotted cream to spread over them.

Amber Pudding

The pudding gets its name from its beautiful golden-amber colour,
which comes from the butter, egg yolks, and candied orange. It
is usually made as one large tart but I find it quite wonderful as
individual tarts. In old recipes the tarts are covered with a lid of
pastry but it is better baked as an open tart so the colour of the
filling can really shine.

110g butter

30g candied orange peel, finely
   chopped

110g icing sugar, plus extra to serve
   (optional)

1 egg

5 egg yolks

Grated zest of ½ orange

FOR THE PASTRY

250g plain flour

100g icing sugar

125g cold butter

Pinch of salt

Grated zest of ½ orange

1 egg

First, make the pastry: combine the flour, sugar, butter, salt and
orange zest in a food processor and blitz until the mixture resembles
breadcrumbs. Add the egg and 1 tablespoon of cold water and blitz
briefly until you have a smooth dough. Refrigerate for at least 1 hour
or overnight.

When ready to use the pastry, roll out on a floured work surface and
use to line six small (8–9cm) tart tins, making sure the pastry fits
tightly in the edges. Use a knife to cut off the excess pastry and then
prick the base with a fork. Freeze for 1 hour.

Preheat the oven to 200°C and place a large baking tray in the oven.

Line the pastry cases with baking paper and baking beans. Place on
the hot baking tray and blind bake for 10–15 minutes or until the edge

is golden brown, then remove the paper and baking beans and bake for a further 5 minutes. Leave to cool.

Meanwhile, make the filling by melting the butter over a low heat – don't let it bubble – then remove from the heat. Put the candied peel in a mortar and use a pestle to bash to a mush.

Add the sugar to the butter and whisk until smooth. Add the egg and yolks, whisking continuously, then add the orange zest and candied orange peel. Leave to rest for at least 15 minutes or while you preheat your oven to 180°C.

Spoon the orange mixture into the pastry cases and bake near the bottom of the oven for 10–15 minutes until a beautiful amber colour.

Serve hot or cold, dusted with icing sugar if you like.

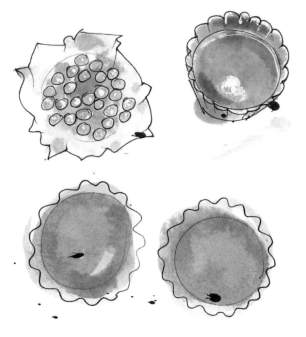

Eve's Pudding

The name refers to the forbidden fruit that Eve plucked from the tree in the Book of Genesis. Today this pudding is baked with a sponge topping but earlier versions were made with breadcrumbs and suet, and were usually boiled. Currants are traditional, but dried barberries were popular in seventeenth-century puddings and they give a great colour. Cointreau can be used instead of lemon juice in the sponge to make a more grown-up version.

50g barberries or currants, soaked overnight in Cointreau or water

3 cooking apples such as Bramley, or Cox

1 tablespoon light brown sugar

150g soft butter

150g demerara sugar

Grated zest and juice of ½ lemon

1 egg

150g plain flour

1 teaspoon baking powder

Caster sugar for sprinkling

Preheat the oven to 180°C.

Generously butter an 18–20cm diameter oven dish or cake tin.

Drain the currants or barberries. Peel, core and chop the apples in chunks no longer than 1.5cm, add to the baking dish and toss with the barberries and the light brown sugar.

Make the sponge by creaming together the butter and sugar, then add the lemon zest and juice (or 1 tablespoon of Cointreau) and beat in the egg. Sift in the flour and baking powder and pour the mixture over the apples. Sprinkle over the caster sugar and bake for 40–50 minutes or until golden brown.

Serve with custard.

Fudge Tart

Also known as butterscotch tart, this was baked in rectangular trays by the dinner ladies at schools and served cold with a big dollop of hot custard on top to melt the fudge. To prevent crystallisation I add a small amount of glucose syrup to the fudge mixture. A small jar will keep for ages and will ensure you never ruin another toffee, fudge or caramel. This recipe makes enough fudge for two tarts with a diameter of 20cm – I find making a smaller quantity of fudge too fiddly. If you don't want two tarts you could spoon the fudge into a baking tray lined with baking paper and leave it to set. Perfect to share with your colleagues!

Shortcrust pastry (page 50)
450g demerara sugar
400g double cream
50g butter
1 tablespoon glucose syrup
1 vanilla pod, seeds only (optional)
Generous pinch of sea salt flakes

To make the pastry, follow the method on page 50. Roll out and line two 20cm diameter tart tins. Blind bake for 10 minutes or until the edge is golden brown, then remove the paper and baking beans and bake for a further 5 minutes to dry out the base. Leave to cool.

Tip the sugar, cream, butter and glucose syrup into a small deep saucepan, with enough space for the mixture to bubble up. Heat on a medium heat to dissolve the sugar, stirring slowly from time to time with a long spatula or wooden spoon. Once the sugar has dissolved, place a sugar thermometer in the pan, increase the heat and bring the mixture to a steady bubble. Keep bubbling, stirring occasionally – stir more frequently once you reach 100°C to stop the sugar from catching

– until the mixture reaches 116°C. This is called the 'soft ball stage' – if you drop a bit of the mixture into cold water, it will form a squidgy ball.

Remove the pan from the heat and leave undisturbed for 5 minutes until the temperature drops to 110°C, then stir in the vanilla seeds, if using, and a good pinch of salt. Keeping the thermometer in the pan, vigorously beat the mixture until it has cooled down to 60°C, then remove the thermometer and beat longer until the fudge is nearly cooled. Then pour the fudge into the tart and leave to set at room temperature.

COOKING TIP If you skip the step where you beat the mixture until it reaches 60°C and pour it into your tart hot, at about 100°C, you will get a mirror finish on the top but the fudge will not harden, so when you serve the tart the filling will run out – slowly but surely. However, I do like the filling runny this way.

Vegetables in puddings

○————————○

Vegetables feature in puddings throughout history. There is a recipe for a sweet carrot pudding baked in a puff pastry crust and flavoured with nutmeg and orange flower water in *The Compleat Cook* by Rebecca Price (1681), and a sweet white potato pudding flavoured with sack – a fortified wine – and candied peel in *The Art of Cookery, Made Plain and Easy* by Hannah Glasse (1747).

During the Second World War, vegetables were never rationed and creating vegetable gardens in every available space was promoted through the 'Dig for Victory' campaign. In 1941, Lord Woolton, the Minister of Food, emphasised the need for self-sustainability in the garden:

'This is a food war. Every extra row of vegetables in allotments saves shipping. The battle on the kitchen front cannot be won without help from the kitchen garden. Isn't an hour in the garden better than an hour in the queue?'

The Ministry of Food created a cartoon figure called Doctor Carrot – dressed in a lab coat and top hat – to motivate housewives to use carrots in cooking. The ministry also spread the story that the Royal Air Force's night flying success was down to the pilots eating lots of carrots – carrot consumption soared because people believed if they also ate a lot of carrots, they might be able to see better during the dreaded blackouts.

They say that carrots helped win the war because of their healthy dose of vitamin A, calcium and beta-carotene – the vegetable also contains fructose and glucose, providing sweetness when sugar was very hard to come by. Children were given carrot sticks instead of lollies and carrots were used in sweet recipes like 'mock apricot' carrot flan, carrot fudge and toffee, carrot jam, carrot cake, a sweet drink called carrolade and, of course, carrot puddings.

A Ministry of Food cookery leaflet gave a recipe for 'War-and-Peace Pudding' – a Christmas pudding made with carrots. It's not that different to carrot cake and always a real hit in my house served with carrot jam and double or clotted cream.

War-and-Peace Pudding

Mix together 1 cupful of flour, 1 cupful of breadcrumbs, half a cupful of suet, half a cupful of mixed dried fruit, and, if you like, a teaspoonful of mixed sweet spice. Then add a cupful of raw potato, a cupful of grated raw carrot and finally a level teaspoonful of bicarbonate of soda dissolved in two tablespoonful of hot water. Mix all together, turn into a well-greased pudding bowl. The bowl should not be more then two-thirds full. Boil or steam for at least 2 hours.

Ministry of Food,
War cookery leaflet no. 4, Carrots

Bedfordshire Clanger

The Bedfordshire clanger is a savoury, portable suet pudding
– rather like a pasty – that was originally the food of farm
labourers. It was also popular in the neighbouring counties of
Buckinghamshire and Hertfordshire. Clangers are often made with
a savoury filling in one end and a sweet filling in the other. It's a
great way of making something fun from leftover meat stew.

300g self-raising flour
100g cold unsalted butter
80g shredded suet
½ teaspoon salt
120ml cold water
1 egg, beaten

FOR THE FILLING
2 eating apples
1 tablespoon light brown sugar
½ teaspoon ground cinnamon
Knob of soft butter
250–300g leftover stew (beef, pork,
  vegetarian – anything works, even
  leftover curry)

Preheat the oven to 200°C and place a baking sheet in the oven to
heat up.

Combine the flour, butter, suet and salt in a large bowl and
rub together using your fingertips until the mixture resembles
breadcrumbs. Add the cold water, stirring the mixture constantly.
Keep adding water until you can press the mixture together into
a smooth dough speckled with suet. Chill in the fridge for at least
an hour. You can prepare the pastry the day before if you're feeling
organised!

To make the apple filling, peel, core and chop the apples and toss in
a saucepan with the sugar, cinnamon and butter. Stir over a medium
heat until soft on the outside but still firm in the centre. Leave to cool.

Place the dough on a lightly floured sheet of baking paper and roll out the pastry to a rectangle of ½cm thickness. Trim the edges and use the trimmings to make a thin wall of dough at the two-thirds point to separate the sweet and savoury fillings.

Brush a 1cm border of beaten egg all around the edges of the dough rectangle. Spread the fillings over one half of your pastry lengthways so that you have enough pastry to bring over the top to cover the fillings. Close the clanger, using the baking paper to lift the pastry. Crimp the ends of the pastry to enclose the filling and score the top with a few slashes so steam can escape during baking.

Use the baking paper to lift the clanger on to the baking sheet and brush all over with beaten egg. Bake for 30–40 minutes or until golden brown.

Cut the clanger lengthways in half to serve so each person has a sweet and savoury portion. Serve hot or cold.

Rhubarb and Apple Crumble

The vivid pink and green of forced Yorkshire rhubarb are irresistible although its colour sadly fades when cooked. My friend Sarka makes a great rhubarb crumble and this is her recipe.

85g wholemeal plain flour
50g rolled oats
65g light brown sugar
½ teaspoon salt
Pinch of freshly ground black pepper
30g flaked almonds
75g butter, softened

FOR THE FILLING
65g light brown sugar
1 tablespoon cornflour
2 apples, cored and diced
8–9 stalks rhubarb, cut into 2cm pieces
3cm piece of fresh ginger, peeled and grated
2 tablespoons rum

Preheat the oven to 180°C and butter an ovenproof dish.

Mix the flour, oats, sugar, salt, black pepper and almonds together in a bowl. Add the butter and rub it in with your fingertips until the mixture resembles breadcrumbs. Press the mixture into a ball and place in the freezer for about 10 minutes.

For the filling, mix together the sugar and cornflour in a large bowl. Add the apples, rhubarb and ginger, and toss until evenly coated. Pour in the rum and toss again.

Put the fruit mixture in the prepared dish and sprinkle the crumble over the top. Bake for 30–40 minutes or until the crumble topping is golden brown and the fruit filling is bubbling.

Let it cool down for at least 15 minutes before serving with thick custard or clotted cream.

Cornflake Tart

People fondly remember eating this at school and at home 20–30 years ago. The cornflake topping also works well on top of a treacle tart, the salty touch of the flakes giving a nice balance to the otherwise incredibly sweet tart. I use butter and lard in this shortcrust pastry, which is traditional, as it creates a shorter pastry, but feel free to use all butter.

FOR THE SHORTCRUST PASTRY
250g plain flour
100g icing sugar
60g cold butter
60g cold lard
Pinch of salt
1 egg

FOR THE FILLING
100g cornflakes
50g butter
25g brown sugar
100g golden syrup
Pinch of salt
2 tablespoons of your favourite jam

To make the pastry, combine the flour, sugar, butter, lard and salt in a food processor and blitz until the mixture resembles breadcrumbs. Add the egg and 1 tablespoon of water and blitz briefly until you have a smooth dough. Refrigerate for at least 1 hour or overnight.

When ready to use the pastry, roll out on a floured work surface and use to line a 22–23cm tart tin, making sure the pastry fits tightly in the edges. Use a knife to cut off the excess pastry and then prick the base with a fork. Freeze for 1 hour. Keep leftover pastry in the freezer.

Preheat the oven to 200°C and place a baking tray in the oven.

Line the pastry case with baking paper and baking beans. Place on the hot baking tray and blind bake for 15 minutes until the edge is golden brown, then remove the paper and baking beans and bake for a further 10 minutes until the base of the crust is golden – the pastry should be fully baked. Leave to cool.

Spread the cornflakes on a baking tray lined with baking paper. Melt the butter in a saucepan then add the sugar, salt and golden syrup and stir until the sugar has dissolved. Pour the hot syrup over the cornflakes in the tray, ensuring that the flakes are completely coated.

Spread the jam over the pastry crust, scoop the sticky cornflake mixture on top and gently spread it out evenly.

Place the tart back in the oven for another 5 minutes, then leave to cool on a wire rack. Serve the same day.

Gypsy Tart

I've searched for the origins of this pudding for a long time and a lot of different stories have been told to me. None of them can be confirmed, so this pudding remains a mystery. Many people still remember it vividly from their schooldays and tell me the pudding used to make their teeth hurt because it was so sweet.

Shortcrust pastry (page 50)
400g evaporated milk, chilled in the
   fridge
310g brown sugar

To make the pastry, follow the method on page 50. Roll out and line a 22–23cm diameter tart tin. Blind bake for 10 minutes or until the edge is golden brown, then remove the paper and baking beans and bake for a further 5 minutes to dry out the base. Leave to cool.

For the filling, whisk the evaporated milk with the brown sugar until evenly mixed and frothy; this takes around 15 minutes, and you need to use an electric whisk.

Pour the mixture into the tart and bake for 20 minutes. When baked the filling will look like it has barely set and it will be very sticky; leave overnight in the fridge to set.

This is the only time I use whipped cream from a can: it is so light that it works perfectly with this incredibly sweet tart.

Hollygog Pudding

This is a type of roly-poly spread with golden syrup and baked in milk. According to Sara Paston-Williams, author of *National Trust Complete Puddings & Desserts*, this pudding originated in the Oxfordshire village of Kiddington.

225g plain flour
Pinch of salt
115g chilled butter
4 tablespoons golden syrup
250ml milk
Icing sugar for dusting

Preheat the oven to 200°C.

Generously butter a baking dish.

In a food processor, pulse the flour, salt and butter until the mixture resembles breadcrumbs. Add 3 tablespoons of cold water and pulse to form a stiff dough. Remove from the food processor and knead briefly then roll out on a sheet of baking paper dusted with icing sugar to form a rectangle about 0.5cm thick. Spread with the golden syrup and roll up like a Swiss roll, using the baking paper to roll up the dough.

Place the roll in the baking dish, sliding it off the baking paper, and pour in enough milk to come just over halfway up the side of the pudding. Bake for 35–45 minutes or until golden.

During baking the milk thickens, leaving a wonderful caramelised skin around the edges. I find it a shame to plate this pudding: I simply place it in the middle of the table and let everyone dive in with their own spoon.

Jam Roly-Poly

This pudding has had many names, from dead man's arm to shirt sleeve pudding, but everyone knows it as a roly-poly pudding. It can be boiled in a tea towel or pudding cloth, but I prefer to bake it in a large loaf tin.

300g plain flour
130g shredded suet
1 teaspoon baking powder
30g sugar
Pinch of salt
Juice of ½ lemon

200ml milk
2–3 tablespoons raspberry jam, or
    any other preserve you fancy
1 egg, beaten
Caster sugar for sprinkling

Preheat the oven to 200°C.

Combine the flour, suet, baking powder, sugar and salt in a large bowl and mix together well. Add the lemon juice to the milk and start adding it while stirring the mixture constantly. Keep adding the liquid until you can bring the mixture together into a stiff dough.

On a well-floured work surface, gently roll the dough out to form a rectangle about 1cm thick. Trim the edges.

Place the dough on a floured tea towel or a sheet of baking paper, spread the jam over the dough, leaving a border at one end. Starting from the other end, use the tea towel or baking paper to roll up the dough. Carefully place the roll, join-side down, on a piece of baking paper and place the pudding in a loaf tin larger than the roll.

Brush the roll with beaten egg and sprinkle over some caster sugar. Bake for 30–40 minutes until risen and golden.

Serve with custard.

VARIATIONS

Christmas Roly-Poly
Use mincemeat instead of jam and serve with apple compote and
custard.

Roly-Poly Bread and Butter Pudding
If you have any leftover roly-poly, arrange the slices in a baking tray,
pour fresh egg custard (page 16, but use 2 egg yolks, 100ml of milk
and 100ml of cream) around it, sprinkle with caster sugar and bake
at 160°C for 40–50 minutes, so the custard is set but still has a little
wobble. The swirls will look so pretty in their yellow bed of custard.
Serve with some fresh raspberries if you used raspberry jam in the
roly-poly.

Manchester Tart

A favourite school pudding: pastry is spread with raspberry jam, covered with a custard filling flavoured with lemon zest (if you were lucky). Top the tart with a sprinkling of desiccated coconut and a cherry for a truly retro touch.

Shortcrust pastry (page 50)
1 egg
5 egg yolks
200ml milk
200ml double cream

Grated zest of 1 lemon
100g demerara sugar
2–4 tablespoons raspberry jam
Desiccated coconut
2 maraschino cherries (optional)

To make the pastry, follow the method on page 50. Roll out and line two 20cm diameter tart tins. Blind bake for 10 minutes or until the edge is golden brown, then remove the paper and baking beans and bake for a further 5 minutes to dry out the base. Leave to cool.

While the pastry is cooling, whisk the egg and yolks in a large bowl. In a large saucepan, heat the milk and the cream with the lemon zest and sugar, bring to a simmer and stir to ensure the sugar has completely dissolved. Pour a little of the hot milk mixture over the whisked eggs and whisk well – this prepares the eggs for the rest of the hot liquid and will prevent curdling – then continue to add it in batches, whisking continuously until smooth. Pour the mixture back into the saucepan and cook over a low heat until the custard thickens. Leave to cool just a little.

Preheat the oven to 180°C and place a baking tray in the oven.

Spread a tablespoon of jam (or more if you prefer) over each pastry case and pour in the custard.

Place on the hot baking tray and bake for 20–25 minutes until the custard is set but still has a wonderful wobble.

Place on a wire rack, then immediately sprinkle with desiccated coconut so that the tart has a nice topping but isn't completely covered with a snow-white blanket. A maraschino cherry in the middle of each tart is optional.

School puddings

School dinners were provided for poor children in the nineteenth century, when there was a great deal of malnutrition in British cities. After the Second World War the government set up basic nutritional standards for school meals; these were abandoned in the 1980s, leading to a decline in the quality of the food offered to children.

Experiences vary wildly, yet the one good thing about the school lunches of the past according to most Brits I've spoken to was the pudding. The main course was often eaten in dismay and the only thing that kept the children going was the knowledge that after the beige food on their plate there was going to be a proper jam roly-poly, spotted dick, Manchester tart, chocolate concrete with pink or mint custard, or lemon sponge with coconut topping and bright yellow custard. People look back on these puddings with fond memories and tasting them again takes them back to their childhood, safe and warm with a pudding so sweet it hurts your teeth. Of course there were some for whom school puddings were a nightmare: they speak of watery custard and soggy bottoms that would make Mary Berry weep. Everything depended on the women who cooked the meals, affectionately called 'dinner ladies'. Some were great pudding cooks, others were not.

Treacle Tart

An old-fashioned school pudding, and – like Marmite – you either love it or hate it. The treacle tart we know today originated after the invention of the iconic golden syrup in 1881. It is called treacle tart because treacle is a generic term for by-products of the sugar refining process. I like a sweet pastry for this tart; pecans are a nice addition but feel free to leave them out and replace with flour.

450g golden syrup
Grated zest and juice of 1 lemon
½ teaspoon ground ginger
120g fresh breadcrumbs
3 tablespoons double cream
1 egg, beaten

FOR THE PECAN PASTRY
200g plain flour
50g ground roasted pecans
100g icing sugar
1 teaspoon ground cinnamon
Pinch of salt
125g cold butter
1 egg

To make the pastry, follow the method on page 50. Roll out and line a 22cm loose-bottomed tart tin. Blind bake for 10 minutes or until the edge is golden brown, then remove the paper and baking beans and bake for a further 5 minutes to dry out the base. Leave to cool.

To make the filling, melt the golden syrup in a saucepan with the lemon zest and juice and the ginger; don't let the syrup boil. When runny and warm add the breadcrumbs and mix well, then let the mixture stand for 10 minutes. Then add the cream and egg and mix well.

Spoon the filling into the pastry case and bake for 30 minutes. The pastry will be quite dark but this will add flavour.

Pearl Barley Pudding

This fragrant pudding was popular in the eighteenth century. It is a close relative of the Italian *pastiera Napoletana*. Old recipes call for rosewater, but if you're not a fan – it can be very overpowering – you can use orange blossom water instead.

The pastry makes enough for two 20–22cm pies: it works best if you make the full quantity – you can freeze the remaining pastry, or use it to make a Bakewell Pudding (page 68)

50g pearl barley
100ml milk
¼ teaspoon ground mace or nutmeg
Pinch of salt
15g soft butter
175g ricotta
175g icing sugar
2 egg yolks
40g mixed candied citrus peel

1 tablespoon cornflour
½ teaspoon rosewater or orange blossom water
FOR THE QUICK PUFF PASTRY
225g plain flour
½ teaspoon fine salt
240g cold butter
130ml ice-cold water

Make the pudding the day before you want to serve it, so it can chill overnight.

For the pastry, put the flour and salt in a large bowl, or the bowl of a food processor, and put it in the fridge. Cut the butter into small cubes and put it into the freezer, alongside the water, for a few minutes.

Before you start the food processor, toss the butter into the flour and use a knife to stir the mixture so every cube of butter is coated in flour. Give two short pulses of about 1 second, then add half the water, pulse again for three short pulses, then add the rest of the water and pulse six times.

Turn out the dough on to a lightly floured work surface. Don't be alarmed if the dough looks very crumbly and is barely holding together at the edges: it's supposed to be that way. Pat the dough into a brick shape, then use a rolling pin to flatten it out to a rectangle. The dough should be quite rough and very marbled with butter.

Fold the right side of the rectangle to the middle and then fold the left side over, making three layers of pastry. Flatten the dough slightly with the rolling pin, then fold up the bottom third of the dough, then fold the top third over to make a small square of dough.

Flatten the dough slightly, wrap in clingfilm and put it in the fridge for at least 30 minutes.

Boil the pearl barley in water until soft, then strain. Tip the pearl barley back into the saucepan and add the milk, mace or nutmeg, salt and butter. Simmer until the mixture is thick, like risotto.

Tip the ricotta into a large bowl, add the sugar and whisk vigorously until well incorporated. Whisk in the egg yolks, followed by the candied peel. Fold in the cooked pearl barley and combine well. Sift over the cornflour and combine well. Now add the rosewater or orange blossom water, mix well and taste; add more if you think it is needed. Leave the mixture to rest for at least 1 hour.

Preheat the oven to 180°C.

Roll out the puff pastry as thin as you can, then use to line a 20cm diameter pie dish. Spoon in the filling and bake near the bottom of the oven for about 50–60 minutes until golden brown. Leave to cool in the pie dish then transfer to the fridge to serve chilled the next day.

Baked Rice Pudding

Once you've baked a rice pudding in the oven you'll never go back to cooking it in a pan on the hob. Baking creates a stunning blistered golden top and caramelised edges, which everyone in your family will fight for.

In the sixteenth century, cookery writer Thomas Dawson flavoured his rice pudding with orange juice, cinnamon and ginger, which is my preference too. Other historical recipes used dried barberries or currants. The options are endless – rice pudding really is a blank canvas and can be made very special with different flavours.

100g pudding rice
25g butter
450ml milk
450ml double cream, or clotted cream
  for an even richer pudding

50g demerara sugar
½ teaspoon ground cinnamon
1 pinch of ground ginger, or seeds
  scraped from half a vanilla pod
Grated zest of ¼ orange (optional)

Rinse the rice under cold water and drain. Preheat the oven to 160°C. Generously butter a large baking dish or four small ovenproof dishes.

Heat the milk, cream, sugar, spices and orange zest, if using, in a saucepan and add the rice. Simmer for 5 minutes, continuously stirring, then pour the mixture into the oven dish(es).

Bake for 1½–1¾ hours, depending on how golden brown you like your pudding. Let the pudding cool a little before serving.

Any leftovers make a delicious and indulgent breakfast the next day.

Russian Raspberry Pudding

Margaret Costa's *Four Seasons Cookery Book* is one every cook should own. She says this pudding is one of the nicest ways to eat raspberries. She warms the raspberries for a few minutes but I skip that step. You can use defrosted frozen raspberries. Margaret uses soured cream while I use a mixture of double cream and yoghurt: the choice is yours. I whisk the egg whites for an airier finish.

450g raspberries, thawed or fresh
3 tablespoons demerara sugar
250ml double cream
50ml yoghurt

2 eggs, separated
15g plain flour
Caster sugar or icing sugar for
    sprinkling

Preheat the oven to 150°C.

Toss the raspberries in a shallow baking dish, about 20cm x 10cm, and sprinkle with 2 tablespoons of the sugar.

In a bowl, beat the cream, yoghurt, egg yolks, the remaining 1 tablespoon of sugar and the flour. In a separate bowl, whisk the egg whites to stiff peaks and fold into the rest of the batter. Pour the mixture over the raspberries and bake near the top of the oven for 45 minutes until pale golden. Sprinkle with caster sugar or dust with icing sugar and serve.

Semolina Pudding with Quince

When I think of this semolina pudding I see a yellow hug of a pudding with lots of possibilities when it comes to adding fruits and jams. Stir it gently and give it some love: this pudding cannot be rushed or it will end up as stodge. Instead of the quince purée you could use apricot or peach compote or jam.

600ml milk
70g demerara sugar
15g butter, plus extra melted butter
  for greasing
145g semolina
Pinch of salt
Grated zest of 1 lemon
2 eggs

FOR THE QUINCE PURÉE
300g quinces
1 cinnamon stick
1 clove, crushed
Peel of 1 lemon
Caster sugar, equal amount to the
  pulp

First make the quince purée. Chop the quinces (no need to peel them), keeping the pips and cores and tying them in muslin – they contain a lot of pectin. Put the quinces in a large saucepan with the spices, lemon peel and the muslin parcel, then add water to cover the quinces and boil until tender, checking texture with a fork.

Remove the quinces from the saucepan and remove the muslin parcel, the cinnamon, and the clove and lemon peel if you can find them. Using a stick blender, blend the quince to a purée. Weigh the purée and return to the pan. Add the same weight of caster sugar, stir well and boil for 5–6 minutes. Test as for jam (see page 22) Strain through a sieve and leave to cool.

Preheat the oven to 160°C.

Grease two 600–800ml fancy-shaped pudding moulds or cake tins with melted butter.

In a saucepan, bring the milk to a gentle simmer with the sugar and butter. Pour in the semolina, salt and lemon zest and stir until it starts to boil, then turn down the heat to very low, add the eggs one at a time, and continue to stir until the mixture is smooth.

Pour about two-thirds of the semolina mixture into the moulds, make a shallow well and spoon in about 2 tablespoons of quince purée, staying away from the edges, then add the rest of the semolina.

Place the moulds in a deep baking dish or large pan and pour in hot water to come halfway up the sides of the pudding moulds.

Bake for 50–60 minutes and then remove from the oven and leave to rest for about 10 minutes. Loosen the puddings at the sides by pushing gently with your fingers, then unmould by placing a plate on top of each mould and turning them over.

Serve hot or cold with a dollop of quince purée.

Tipsy Pudding

Eliza Acton explains in her book *Modern Cookery for Private Families* (1845) that Tipsy Cake or Tipsy Pudding was made by soaking a tall sponge called a Savoy cake in brandy. Mrs Beeton suggests using a sweet wine to soak the cake. It was placed on a salver and studded with blanched almonds cut into spikes, and served in slices in a pool of custard.

Moulded cakes like this were extremely different to bake in the temperamental ovens of the nineteenth century, so they showed off the skills of the pastry cook. With intricate cake pans it is better to use lard or oil to grease the mould so the cake will release better.

4 eggs, separated
100g caster sugar
Grated zest of 1 lemon or 1 orange
45g plain flour
45g cornflour

Pinch of salt
Icing sugar to dust the mould
Brandy, madeira or any sweet wine or liqueur
Sliced almonds

Make the cake two days before you want to serve the pudding to let the cake dry out, leaving it covered by a glass dome or tea towel.

Preheat the oven to 200°C.

Grease your mould with oil or butter.

Place the egg yolks in a small bowl and the whites in a large bowl. Whisk the egg whites to stiff peaks and then gradually add the sugar, one teaspoon at a time, whisking vigorously until stiff and glossy.

Add a teaspoon of the mixture to the egg yolks, add the zest and whisk. Now transfer the egg yolk mixture to the whites and fold in. Sift the flour and cornflour over the mixture, add a pinch of salt and fold in, making sure the mixture is well combined but keeping as much of the airiness as possible.

Dust your greased mould with cornflour, removing the excess by turning the mould upside down and tapping, then dust with icing sugar.

Spoon the batter into the mould, then place in the bottom of the oven if you are using a tall mould, or in the middle if using a normal mould or cake tin. Bake for 30–40 minutes until the top is golden brown.

Leave to rest in the mould for 10 minutes then unmould and leave to cool completely on a wire rack. The cake will look very pale.

To serve, place the cake on a wire rack in a large tray. Gently drizzle over the alcohol, starting from the top and moving around the sides, then wait to see if alcohol starts to drip out: when this happens the tipsy pudding is ready, as the cake is saturated. Decorate the cake by pushing the almond pieces all over it. Serve sliced, with custard.

Bakewell Pudding

I've travelled to Bakewell in pursuit of the true recipe for Bakewell pudding but found that historical cookbooks tell the story far better. The first recipe for a Bakewell Pudding appeared in print in 1836 but the pudding is even older than this, finding its origins in the sweetmeat puddings of the eighteenth century. Sweetmeat was the name for any kind of preserve, usually candied peel, and later jams – the preserve or jam remains an important part of the pudding today. Some old Bakewell Pudding recipes use lemon or bitter almond to flavour the pudding, others use spices like nutmeg, or a liqueur.

Quick puff pastry (page 60)

100g butter

25g apricot kernels (or a few drops of almond essence)

1 teaspoon rosewater

110g demerara sugar, powdered in a food processor

4 egg yolks

1 egg

2 tablespoons raspberry jam

50g candied lemon peel, cut into strips

Make the pastry, wrap and chill.

Melt the butter, making sure it doesn't start to bubble and burn; leave it to cool down.

Blanch the apricot kernels by immersing them in boiling water for a few minutes. Now peel off the skins, which should come off easily, if not, soak longer.

Using a mortar and pestle, pound the blanched apricot kernels with the rosewater; this will release the heavenly scent of fresh marzipan. Transfer to a bowl and whisk in the clarified butter and the sugar, whisking until creamy, then whisk in the eggs one by one.

Preheat the oven to 180°C.

Roll out the puff pastry as thin as you can, then use to line two 22cm diameter enamel plates. Spread the raspberry jam over the base, leaving a 2cm border all round. Neatly arrange strips of candied lemon peel over the jam, then gently pour in the filling mixture.

Bake near the bottom of the oven for 15 minutes, then move to the middle of the oven and bake for 15 minutes until golden brown.

Serve warm or cold. This recipe makes two puddings, or several smaller puddings.

Kentish Cherry Batter Pudding

Cherry batter pudding is a sweet and fruity variation of a Yorkshire pudding. It is associated with the county of Kent where historically there were a large number of cherry orchards. It can be made with apples to create a Nottingham pudding; apricots and peaches work well too.

110g plain flour
Pinch of salt
3 eggs
280ml milk
Sunflower oil or lard for baking
Icing sugar for dusting

FOR THE BRAISED CHERRIES
300g fresh cherries, stoned
20g demerara sugar
150ml unsweetened apple juice or
    water

To make the braised cherries, put them in a saucepan with the sugar, apple juice or water and simmer until the cherries are tender. Using a slotted spoon, remove them from the sauce and set aside.

To make the batter, sift the flour and salt into a large bowl and add the eggs and milk, whisking until smooth. Leave the batter to rest for 30 minutes or so.

Preheat the oven to 250°C or as high as your oven goes.

Pour a 1cm layer of sunflower oil or lard into a baking dish or muffin tin and set it in the middle of the hot oven. Place a larger tray underneath, to prevent a smoky kitchen in case the oil drips.

When the oil is hot, swiftly but carefully remove the tray from the oven and pour the batter into the dish or muffin holes and then add a generous amount of the drained cherries.

Return the dish to the oven and don't open the oven door until the pudding is golden brown and puffed up: this should take about 25–30 minutes. Meanwhile, put the remaining cherries back in the sauce and reduce over a low heat until about two-thirds of the sauce remains.

Serve the pudding warm, with the sauce drizzled over, dusted with icing sugar.

Queen of Puddings

Using breadcrumbs to thicken a custard is an old technique. You can add the warmed jam and the meringue topping when the custard is lightly set – about 25 minutes – and return the pudding to the oven for 15 minutes or until the meringue is crisp and lightly browned, but today it is fashionable to pipe a perfect snow-white meringue and serve it as is. For the unbaked version, you will need to use pasteurised egg whites or make an Italian meringue (page 8).

4 egg yolks
600ml milk
20g caster sugar
Grated zest of 1 lemon
25g butter, plus extra for greasing
80g fresh breadcrumbs
2 tablespoons raspberry jam

FOR THE MERINGUE TOPPING
4 pasteurised egg whites
225g caster sugar
Pinch of cream of tartar

Preheat the oven to 180°C.

Generously butter an 18cm diameter baking dish.

Whisk the egg yolks in a large bowl. Put the milk, sugar and lemon zest in a saucepan, bring to a simmer (do not boil) and stir in the butter.

Pour a little of the hot milk mixture into the egg yolks and whisk thoroughly. Gradually whisk in the rest of the hot milk until you have a smooth custard.

Put a layer of breadcrumbs in the buttered dish, then pour over the custard sauce and let it rest for 15 minutes.

Place the baking dish in a roasting tin and pour in boiling water to come halfway up the dish. Carefully place the tin in the oven and bake for 35 minutes.

Towards the end of the baking time, make the meringue topping. Using an electric whisk, whisk the egg whites to soft peaks. Add the sugar a tablespoon at a time, followed by the cream of tartar, and continue to whisk until the meringue is stiff and glossy.

Remove the pudding from the oven and spread the raspberry jam carefully over the custard layer. Now either spoon the meringue over the hot pudding, or scoop into a piping bag and make fancy swirls. Use a blowtorch to give some colour to the meringue or leave it white as snow.

Bread Puddings

Hot Cross Bun and Butter Pudding

A great way to use up any type of leftover buns, bread or brioche.

Butter, for greasing and spreading
2–3 day-old hot cross buns
25g currants, soaked in water or rum
  overnight (optional)
350ml milk
50ml double cream
2 tablespoons demerara sugar

1 mace blade or the seeds scraped
  from a vanilla pod
4 egg yolks
2 teaspoons caster sugar, for
  sprinkling

Preheat the oven to 180°C.

Generously butter a large baking dish. Cut the buns into 1cm thick slices and butter on one side. Arrange a layer of bun slices, buttered side up, in the baking dish. If using currants, scatter them over the top of the buns.

To make the custard, gently warm the milk, cream, demerara sugar and mace or vanilla in a saucepan over a low heat. Whisk the egg yolks in a bowl, add a little of the warm milk mixture and whisk well, then gradually add the rest of the milk mixture, whisking constantly.

Carefully pour the custard over the buns and sprinkle with the sugar. Bake for 20–25 minutes until the custard has set and the tops are golden brown.

This is scrumptious with a handful of crushed raspberries, but then raspberries go with just about any pudding.

Shooting puddings

At the fourteenth-century moated castle of Bodiam in East Sussex a local archery group had a peculiar tradition of shooting arrows at Christmas puddings. The archers would gather each January in what is thought to have been the medieval jousting field of the castle.

This custom began around three decades ago when a Christmas pudding manufacturer reduced the amount of preservatives in its Christmas puddings, resulting in mouldy puddings. The folk from the area decided to use the mouldy puddings as archery targets and so the Bodiam Castle Christmas Pudding Clout was born. However, I find it hard to believe that the puddings went mouldy as a result of reducing preservatives, as the nature of a Christmas pudding is that it doesn't go mouldy when stored well because of the alcohol it contains; it can either mature or become as dry as a stone. I have Christmas puddings that are over two years old and no mould has developed. In fact I think a matured Christmas pudding is the best and tend to buy one for the next year.

In recent years, the archery targets weren't actually Christmas puddings – it would have been a waste of good pudding – but the winner of the tournament took home a wooden effigy of a Christmas pudding. Those of you with a passion for classic Christmas pudding can plan a winter visit to Bodiam where you can enjoy this rich pudding after lunch at the castle's Wharf Tearoom throughout December. A walk in the Sussex countryside or along the seafront will deal with the extra calories in no time.

Wet Nelly

This recipe is from Speke Hall, an impressive Tudor manor house near Liverpool. It is a moist version of a Nelson cake, hence the name Wet Nelly, and is better known as bread pudding. Similar recipes are found in many parts of the world, as a way of using leftover bread or buns. I like to finish this pudding off with chocolate icing as is traditional in my home region of Flanders, but you can leave it plain.

Loaf of white bread (day-old-becoming-dry is perfect for this recipe), crusts cut off and cut into chunky squares
750ml warm milk
100g butter
140g brown sugar
500g mixed fruit
2 teaspoons mixed spice
3 eggs

In a large bowl, soak the bread in the milk for at least 4 hours and preferably overnight.

Preheat the oven to 180°C.

Add all the other ingredients to the soaked bread, mix together well and pour into a greased, deep-sided roasting tin. Bake for 1–1¼ hours until soft but springy to the touch.

Delicious served hot with custard or cold with a cup of tea.

Summer Pudding

Summer pudding became popular during the nineteenth century when it was served in spas to ladies taking the waters; it was suggested as a way to avoid heavier pastry-based puddings.

650g raspberries
150g blackberries
100g redcurrants or blueberries

50g demerara sugar
Loaf of white bread, crusts cut off
    and cut into 1cm thick slices

Lightly grease a 17cm diameter pudding basin, charlotte mould or deep cake tin and line with clingfilm. Leave enough clingfilm overhanging the edges to cover the pudding when filled.

Put all the berries in a saucepan, add the sugar and heat gently for 2–3 minutes to get the crimson juices running. If using frozen berries they will need a little longer to stew. Let the berries cool in the pan.

Cut a round out of a slice of bread to fit the bottom of the pudding basin and a larger one to cover the top. Now trim the remaining bread slices into a slight trapezium shape to fit the sloping sides of the bowl. If your bowl is straight or you are using a cake tin or charlotte mould, just cut the bread into fingers.

Line the basin or mould with the bread, making sure there are no gaps. Spoon the cooled berries into the bread-lined basin, reserving as much of the juice in the saucepan as you can manage.

Cover the pudding with the large round of bread to completely cover the fruit. Spoon over some of the reserved juice to cover the bread. Reserve any remaining juice for serving.

Cover the pudding with the overhanging clingfilm, then place a plate on top and put a weight on the plate: I use a tin of tomatoes or beans. Refrigerate overnight.

When ready to serve, open the clingfilm, place a serving plate on top of the basin and invert. Serve with clotted cream, vanilla ice cream or whipped cream.

Milk Puddings

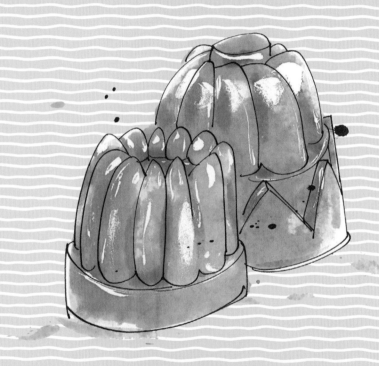

Almond Blancmange with Gooseberry Compote

Blancmange means 'white food' and is one of the oldest dishes in European cuisine. The earliest forms of blancmange were made with white meat or white fish for fast days. In more recent centuries, recipes were based on almonds. The tartness of the gooseberries is perfect with this creamy almond blancmange. It's also good served with thin crisp butter biscuits.

FOR THE BLANCMANGE
60g almonds
1 teaspoon rosewater
400ml milk
400ml double cream
2 tablespoons white sugar
8 gelatine leaves

FOR THE GOOSEBERRY COMPOTE
500g gooseberries, topped and tailed
70g caster sugar

To blanch the almonds, put them in a bowl and pour boiling water over them, then rinse under cold water and dry them in a clean tea towel to rub off the skins.

Using a mortar and pestle, pound the blanched almonds with the rosewater until you get a purée. Put the milk and cream in a saucepan, add the almond purée and sugar and bring to the boil, then remove from the heat and leave to cool slightl. Transfer to the fridge and leave overnight.

For the compote, put the gooseberries in a saucepan with the sugar and 2 tablespoons of water, bring to a simmer and cook gently for about 10 minutes until the gooseberries are soft. Leave to cool.

The next day, strain the cream mixture into a saucepan and discard the almond pulp; bring the cream to a simmer. Soak the gelatine briefly in enough water to cover the leaves, until softened. Then gently squeeze the gelatine to remove the water and stir it into the warm cream mixture until fully dissolved.

Leave to cool, but don't leave it long enough to set. Pour it into a wet mould, or eight small moulds, and put it in the fridge for at least 6 hours or preferably overnight.

To unmould, wet one of your hands and use it to loosen the blancmange. Turn out on to a wet plate (if the plate is wet, you can easily move the blancmange around if necessary).

Serve with the gooseberry compote and thin butter biscuits.

A mess of a pudding

Eton mess was first mentioned in print in 1896 when 'Eton Mess aux Fraises' was served to Queen Victoria at the royal table in Marlborough House in London, as recorded in the 1896 book *Marlborough House and its Occupants: Present and past* by Arthur H. Beavan. But why is it called Eton mess? The story goes that a pudding was dropped on the floor at an Eton versus Harrow cricket match in the late nineteenth century and instead of wasting it, quick thinkers scooped it up off the floor and plated it as individual servings. Unlikely as it sounds, such an event was the making of a new dish at Massimo Bottura's restaurant Osteria Francescana, a three-Michelin-star restaurant in Italy. When a member of staff dropped a lemon tart, a new deconstructed lemon tart dish was born, which was named 'Oops, I dropped the lemon tart'.

Eton Mess

Eton Mess is ideal for serving to large parties – you can use a wooden board and create a huge, beautiful mess. Mixing double cream with thick yoghurt makes the cream just slightly lighter. The passion fruit and mango coulis adds a great colour contrast.

---

6 egg whites

300g caster sugar, plus 1 tablespoon for sprinkling

Pinch of cream of tartar

500–600g (total weight) fresh strawberries, raspberries and blackberries

250ml double cream

1 tablespoon icing sugar

250g Greek yoghurt or skyr

3 tablespoons shelled, unsalted pistachios, chopped

FOR THE MANGO AND PASSION FRUIT COULIS

6 passion fruit

160ml mango juice

3 tablespoons sugar

Preheat the oven to 130°C.

Line two baking sheets with baking paper.

Using an electric whisk, whisk the egg whites to soft peaks. Add the sugar a tablespoon at a time, followed by the cream of tartar, still whisking, until the meringue is stiff and glossy. Scoop on to the baking sheets, spread roughly so you're left with peaks, and bake for 1 hour 10 minutes, or until crisp on the outside. Leave to cool.

To make the coulis, scoop out the pulp and seeds of the passion fruit into a saucepan, pour in the mango juice, sugar and 100ml of water and bring to the boil. Reduce the heat and simmer for about 5 minutes or until the liquid has thickened slightly. Leave for a few minutes then strain to remove the seeds. Allow to cool fully before pouring into a piping bag; place in the fridge until needed.

Halve or quarter the strawberries depending on how large they are, halve the blackberries and leave the raspberries whole.

Whip the double cream with the icing sugar until soft peaks form, then fold in the yoghurt or skyr.

Place one big meringue on a large board, break it up just a little so it looks like you dropped it, then add half of the cream mixture in blobs followed by half of the fruit. Break the other meringue into pieces and place them on top, followed by the rest of the cream in blobs and the remaining fruit.

Get your piping bag with coulis out of the fridge and snip off a corner now have fun piping that coulis all over the mess, Jackson Pollock-style.

Sprinkle with the pistachios and a tablespoon of caster sugar and present with a couple of serving spoons so people can help themselves.

Arctic Roll

This is a great retro pudding and ideal for making ahead of a
dinner party. The trick is to get the ice cream just soft enough
to shape. You can use shop-bought ice cream and jam or make
your own.

Vanilla ice cream, one 500ml tub
3–4 tablespoons strawberry jam
2 handfuls of unsalted pistachios,
  shelled and chopped
FOR THE STRAWBERRY JAM
200g strawberries, chopped
150g jam sugar
Juice of 1 lemon

FOR THE SPONGE
4 eggs, separated
100g caster sugar, plus extra for
  sprinkling
Grated zest of 1 lemon or 1 orange
45g plain flour
45g cornflour
Pinch of salt

To make the strawberry jam, follow the instructions for elderberry
jam (page 22), but don't cook the fruit first, just add the sugar and
lemon juice to the chopped strawberries, bring to the boil over a low
heat, stirring occasionally until the sugar has dissolved, then boil
hard for 5–8 minutes before testing for set. The jam should not be too
runny. Let the jam cool completely and if possible chill overnight.

Preheat the oven to 200°C.

Line a Swiss roll tin with baking paper and sprinkle with caster sugar.
To make the sponge, whisk the egg whites in a large bowl until they
form stiff peaks. Add in the caster sugar, a teaspoon at a time, until
you have a meringue. Add a teaspoon of meringue mixture to the egg
yolks, add the zest and whisk together. Then add the egg yolk mixture
to the meringue and mix well. Sift the flour, then fold the flour and
cornflour into the meringue, making sure it is well mixed but keeping
in as much air as possible.

Spoon the batter into the Swiss roll tin and level the surface with a spatula. Bake for 6–8 minutes until pale golden.

Take the ice cream out of the freezer so it becomes easier to scoop.

Turn out the sponge on to a sheet of baking paper, trim the sides, then roll up and set aside for a few minutes.

Unroll the sponge, spread with the jam and scatter over the pistachios. Dollop the ice cream swiftly on to the sponge then roll up to form a tube, tidy the edges by pressing in the ice cream if some is peeping out and wrap the baking paper around it, twisting each end as if it were a sweetie wrapper. Transfer to the freezer for 3 hours. Take out about 20 minutes before serving – less if it is a hot summer day.

Trinity Burnt Cream

Also known as crème brûlée, old recipes for versions of this pudding are found in various parts of Britain and Europe. Its association with Trinity College, Cambridge goes back to at least the nineteenth century.

6 egg yolks
1 teaspoon rice flour
800ml milk
1 cinnamon stick

2 teaspoons candied peel, finely
   chopped
6 teaspoons golden caster sugar

Preheat the oven to 180°C.

Whisk the egg yolks thoroughly in a large bowl and sift in the rice flour. Put the milk in a saucepan over a low heat with the cinnamon and candied peel. Bring to a simmer, then take the pan off the heat.

Take out the cinnamon stick. Pour a small amount of warm milk into the egg yolks and whisk thoroughly, then gradually add the rest of the milk, whisking constantly until you have a smooth custard.

Place six 150ml ramekins in a large baking dish and spoon the warm custard mixture into the ramekins. Place the dish in the oven and carefully pour in enough hot water to come about 1.5cm up the sides.

Bake for 50 minutes or until the custard is set but still has a gentle wobble. Let the ramekins cool and then transfer them to the fridge.

When you are ready to serve, gently spread a teaspoon of sugar over each custard. Gently burn the sugar by holding the flame of a blowtorch just above it and moving the torch around until the sugar is caramelised.

Everlasting Syllabub

Syllabubs were all the rage in the eighteenth century. The white frothy syllabub was served in specially designed glasses and topped with a sprig of rosemary. A regular syllabub would soon separate: the creamy froth would be spooned off, leaving a boozy drink. Everlasting syllabubs did not separate as quickly and were often used as a layer in a trifle – more modern trifles use whipped cream instead.

425ml double cream
50g icing sugar
80ml lemon juice
125ml white wine, such as a sweet
   Riesling
60ml sherry or Madeira

Using an electric whisk on low speed, beat together the cream and sugar. Combine the lemon juice with the alcohol and add to the cream, whisking constantly until it is thick. This can be done by hand but it needs at least 10–15 minutes of whisking.

Scoop into glasses or small jars and serve. This is also very good to spoon over fruit compote or fresh fruit salad.

Passion Fruit and Mango Fool

A fool is a pudding made by blending puréed tart fruit with
sweetened cream. The origin of the name is lost in time, and
the fool as we know it today dates from the eighteenth century.
Although gooseberry and raspberry are traditional, I rather like
passion fruit and mango. I sometimes add some broken pieces of
meringue for a contrasting texture.

8 passion fruit
2 teaspoons caster sugar
500ml double cream, whipped
2 mangoes, cut into cubes

Scoop out the pulp and seeds of four passion fruit and strain to
remove the seeds.

Scoop out the pulp and seeds of the other four passion fruit without
straining and set aside.

Add the sugar to the cream and whip to soft peaks; taste and add
more if you have a sweet tooth.

Stir half of the cream into the strained passion fruit so you get a nice
yellow colour.

Divide the remaining cream among six glasses or small jars. Layer
two thirds of the mango cubes on the cream, then add the passion
fruit cream. Top with the remaining passion fruit pulp and a few
cubes of mango.

Trifles

Italian Trifle

Zuppa inglese is the Italian version of trifle. The name translates as 'English soup' – but there are many theories as to how it got this name. A simple explanation could be that *inzuppare* means 'to dunk, or soak' – after all, an essential part of the trifle is to soak your cake in alcohol. For *zuppa inglese* the alcohol used is Alchermes, a bright red spiced liqueur. One of my dearest friends, Giulia, is an Italian cookery writer and teacher who lives in the rolling Tuscan countryside. This is her recipe and there really is none better.

1 litre milk
1 vanilla pod, split
4 eggs
8 tablespoons sugar
4 tablespoons cornflour
100g dark chocolate, chopped, plus 100g to decorate

Alchermes, cherry brandy, or another sweet spiced liqueur
Sponge fingers or sponge cake (around 12 fingers)
Whipped cream (optional)

Heat the milk in a large saucepan with the vanilla pod; as soon as it starts to simmer, remove the pan from the heat and leave the vanilla to infuse in the milk.

In a large bowl, whisk the eggs with the sugar, then sift in the cornflour and whisk well until evenly blended.

Remove the vanilla pod and pour a small splash of warm milk into the egg mixture, whisk well, then pour in the rest of the milk, whisking continuously. Pour the mixture back into the saucepan and bring back to a simmer over a low heat, continuing to whisk until it starts to thicken, about 5 minutes.

Remove the custard from the heat and divide it between two bowls. Toss 100g of chocolate into one bowl and whisk until smooth.

Pour 20ml of Alchermes into a deep plate and briefly dip the sponge fingers in the liqueur on both sides, adding more liqueur if needed.

Construct the zuppa inglese in a large bowl or in individual glasses, by making several layers of custard, soaked sponge fingers and chocolate custard, finishing with plain custard. Sprinkle with chopped chocolate and leave in the fridge for a few hours before serving.

VARIATIONS
Instead of adding the chocolate you can add a layer of whipped cream just before serving. You can then, of course, still add some chocolate.

If you can't find Alchermes, you can use cherry brandy. It will taste similar but won't have the same bright colour.

Retro Trifle

A trifle constructed in a large glass bowl is incredibly pleasing. Summer trifles are good with strawberries, while winter versions can be made with preserved peaches. Sponge fingers and ratafia or amaretti biscuits are traditional, but slices of Swiss roll make for a pretty variation. I am not fond of jelly in a trifle, but feel free to add if you are a jelly lover.

500ml double cream, whipped
25g icing sugar 1 pack of sponge
  fingers
1 pack of amaretti biscuits
Brandy or sherry for drizzling
500g strawberries, hulled and
  halved or
500g preserved peaches or nectarines,
  halved
Everlasting Syllabub (page 92)

FOR THE CUSTARD
5 egg yolks
250ml milk
250ml double cream
25g caster sugar
1 vanilla pod, split
1 tablespoon cornflour, mixed with
  1 tablespoon milk

First, make the custard. Whisk the egg yolks in a large bowl. In a saucepan, bring the milk, cream, sugar and vanilla pod to a simmer. Remove the vanilla pod and pour a little of the hot cream mixture into the egg yolks while whisking vigorously. Continue to add the cream mixture bit by bit, whisking until smooth. Pour the mixture back into the saucepan, add the cornflour, and cook over a low heat until the custard thickens. When thick and smooth, transfer to a jug or bowl and leave to cool.

Meanwhile prepare your syllabub (page 92) and whip your double cream to stiff peaks with the icing sugar. Place in the fridge until ready to assemble the trifle.

In a 30cm diameter trifle bowl, make a layer of sponge fingers and drizzle generously with brandy or sherry, then follow this with a layer of around 10–12 amaretti biscuits. Pour the cold custard over the biscuits and put in the fridge for about 15 minutes.

Add a layer of fruit over the custard.

If you like, add a jelly layer at this point: pour in cooled but not set jelly over the fruit and refrigerate until set.

Scoop the syllabub on top of the fruit. Add another layer of sponge fingers and a couple of crushed amaretti, if you still have some left, and sprinkle with brandy or sherry. Add a layer of whipped cream and decorate the top with sliced or halved strawberries or your other chosen fruit. Leave in the fridge for an hour, or up to 8 hours, so the flavours can develop.

Whim-Wham

A whim-wham means something fanciful and centuries ago it was the name for a very simple trifle.

Everlasting syllabub (page 92)
Sweet sherry or Madeira
FOR THE SPONGE FINGERS
4 eggs, separated
100g caster sugar, plus extra for
    sprinkling

Grated zest of 1 lemon or 1 orange
45g plain flour
45g cornflour
Pinch of salt

Start this pudding one day in advance by making the sponge fingers.

Preheat the oven to 200°C.

Line two baking trays with baking paper. Make the sponge mixture (page 89) and spoon the mixture into a large piping bag with a 1cm round nozzle. Stick the baking paper to the baking trays using a pea-sized quantity of mixture in each corner. Pipe finger lengths of the mixture on to one of the baking trays, leaving a little space between each one. Bake for 6–8 minutes until pale golden. Leave to cool on a wire rack while you bake the next batch. Leave to cool completely.

Make the syllabub.

To assemble, make a layer of sponge fingers in a wide shallow bowl and drizzle with sherry or Madeira. You will not need all the sponge fingers; freeze any left over. Top with the syllabub and leave in the fridge for 1 hour before serving.

Serve with chopped soft fruit or berries, or flaked almonds.

103

Latvian Rye and Cranberry Trifle

Latvia's traditional trifle is is made by layering their iconic dark rye bread with cream and their traditional fresh cheese (similar to ricotta) and tart red cranberries or lingonberries.

350g fresh or frozen cranberries or lingonberries
1 tablespoon caster sugar
300g dry dark rye breadcrumbs
Alcohol (optional); I used sloe gin which was incredible

300g double cream
1 tablespoon icing sugar
100g ricotta

First make the cranberry coulis. Keeping some fruit aside for decoration, simmer the rest in a pan with the caster sugar, adding a little water from time to time until they have the texture of apple sauce. The ideal consistency should be thick enough to leave a line in the pan when you go through it with your spoon, yet runny enough that it drops from the spoon. Leave to cool. Add sugar to taste.

Lightly toast the rye crumbs in a dry heavy-bottomed pan, then leave to cool. Drizzle them with the alcohol, if using.

Whisk the cream with the icing sugar until it forms stiff peaks then fold in the ricotta. Fill a piping bag and place in the fridge to firm up.

Take four or six glasses and make a generous layer of breadcrumbs in each, then add a layer of the coulis. Pipe a layer of cream on top of the coulis. Add another layer of crumbs, then coulis, then cream until your glasses are full – make sure you end up with cream on top.

Place in the fridge for a few hours or overnight so the flavours can blend. Before serving, decorate with the berries you kept aside.

Colchester Tapioca Pudding

This recipe is inspired by a 1914 book called *Pot-Luck* by May Byron. She includes a layer of custard on top of the tapioca and suggests colouring the meringue pale pink. Whole (full fat) dairy milk is traditional but I like to cook the tapioca with coconut milk, which works beautifully with rosewater.

100g tapioca

650ml milk or coconut milk

25g caster sugar

Rosewater, to taste

FOR THE FRUIT LAYER

450g fresh fruit, such as raspberries

or mango, or compote made with 450g fruit and 50g sugar

FOR THE MERINGUE

5 pasteurised egg whites

1 teaspoon lemon juice

300g caster sugar

Put the tapioca and milk in a saucepan and leave to soak for 1 hour. After soaking, place the saucepan on a low heat, add the sugar, and bring to a simmer while continuously stirring until softened and thickened, about 10 minutes. Add the rosewater, starting with one small drop and adding more to taste. Leave to cool.

If using fresh fruit, chop into small pieces. To make compote, tip the fruit and sugar into a saucepan and cook on a low heat for 5–10 minutes until the fruit is lightly cooked but still holding its shape. Leave to cool.

Make the meringue by whisking the egg whites with the lemon juice until they form stiff peaks. Add the sugar one teaspoon at a time, whisking until thick and glossy. Transfer to a piping bag.

Make a layer of fruit in a large bowl, or six individual bowls, add a layer of tapioca, then pipe over the meringue, which you can leave snow white, or brown using a blowtorch.

Charlotte Royale with Soft Cheese Filling

Charlottes Royale are usually filled with a set custard or a mousse studded with soft fruit. I find a fresh cheese filling works very well. You can use any soft fruit in the filling. If you like, you can make your own Swiss roll using the recipe on page 89.

250g strawberry or raspberry Swiss roll

300g double cream

1 tablespoon icing sugar

100g ricotta, curd cheese or drained cottage cheese

20g candied orange peel, finely chopped

1 tin of apricots in syrup or stewed fresh apricots, well drained (drained weight about 230g)

4–5 broken sponge fingers or a handful of amaretti biscuits, lightly crushed

Cut the Swiss roll into 1cm thick slices. Line a 2-litre pudding basin with clingfilm, leaving plenty of clingfilm hanging over the rim to cover the pudding later on.

Whisk the cream with the icing sugar then add the ricotta and mix evenly. Fold in the candied peel and the fruit and finally the sponge fingers or amaretti biscuits.

Arrange the slices of Swiss roll all around the pudding basin, leaving no gaps. Scoop in the cheese mixture. If you have some leftover Swiss roll you will be able to cover the base too.

Wrap the clingfilm over the pudding and place a small plate on top followed by something to weigh it down, such as a tin of beans.

Leave in the fridge for at least 1 hour. To serve, open the clingfilm and invert the pudding on to a serving plate. Remove the clingfilm, slice and serve.

Lemon Posset Ice Cream
with Brandy Snaps

A posset is one of the oldest puddings – it started out as a hot spiced drink with milk and eggs curdled with sweet wine, but today it is a lighter, much more elegant pudding. Here it is frozen and paired with lemon curd for a zingy variation on a trifle. The brandy snaps are a reminder of the pudding's boozy past.

500ml double cream

1 teaspoon icing sugar

FOR THE LEMON CURD (MAKES 650G)

225g caster sugar

Finely grated zest of 2 large lemons
(use the lemons you are juicing)

225ml lemon juice

3 whole eggs

3 egg yollks

Pinch of sea salt

100g soft butter

FOR THE BRANDY SNAPS

50g butter

1 teaspoon lemon juice

1 teaspoon brandy

50g demerara sugar

50g golden syrup

50g plain flour

¼ teaspoon ground coriander

First make the lemon curd. Put the sugar in a heatproof bowl and add the lemon zest, then the eggs and whisk to combine well. Whisk in the lemon juice a little at a time until fully incorporated.

Place the bowl over a pan of simmering water and keep on a low heat. Stir continuously with a whisk until the curd has the consistency of custard; this will take about 8 minutes. Take the pan off the heat and whisk in the salt, then add the butter in batches, whisking vigorously until smooth. Keep 250g of curd aside for this recipe and transfer the remaining 400g to a sterilised jar or airtight container to cool.

Whisk the cream and icing sugar together until floppy, then fold in 250g of the cold lemon curd. Put the mixture in your ice-cream maker and proceed according to your machine's instructions. Alternatively, freeze a cake tin, pour in the cream mixture, place back in the freezer and stir every 30 minutes until it thickens and you have ice cream.

To make the brandy snaps, preheat the oven to 180°C and line a baking tray with baking paper. Put the butter, lemon juice, brandy, sugar and golden syrup in a saucepan over a low heat and stir until the sugar has dissolved. Transfer to a bowl and leave to cool.

When cool, add the flour and coriander and mix well so there aren't any flour pockets left. Drop a teaspoonful of batter on to the baking paper and then use the back of the spoon to smooth it out into a finger shape, making sure the mixture is evenly spread. Bake until the biscuits have a beautiful caramel colour, which will take 5–8 minutes depending on your oven. Leave on the baking tray for 1 minute, then transfer to a wire rack to cool and become crisp.

To assemble, take the ice cream out of the freezer 10–15 minutes in advance so it is easy to spoon.

Spoon a teaspoon of the leftover lemon curd into six serving glasses, followed by a layer of ice cream, then another layer of lemon curd and a layer of ice cream. Return to the freezer for at least 10 minutes, then serve with a brandy snap in each glass.

Index

ACKNOWLEDGEMENTS

○————————————○

I would like to thank the National Trust for inviting me to write this book. Thanks to the National Trust properties for allowing us to include their pudding recipes and to Sara Paston-Williams for the National Trust book of puddings she wrote many years ago.

Thank you food historian Dr Annie Gray for sharing your knowledge about Churchill's cook and sending me a couple of her pudding recipes to explore. I do love our pudding talks.

Thanks to all the kind people who told me their pudding-related stories and treasured pudding memories – it appears that rhubarb and apple crumble is currently Britain's favourite pudding.

Thanks to my dearest friends and my lovely husband for supporting me and eating a lot of pudding.

Thank you to Peter, Lucy and Komal from Pavilion Books.

Further Reading

○————————————○

Sara Edington, *Classic British Cooking* (National Trust Books, 2018)

Charles Elmé Francatelli, *The Modern Chef* (1846)

Hannah Woolley, *The Queen-like Closet* (1672)

Georgina Landemare, *Recipes from No.10* (Collins, 1959)

Sara Paston-Williams, *National Trust Complete Puddings and Desserts* (National Trust Books, 2014)